# Connecting The Dots

## Social Media Marketing and Business Success

### Andrew K. Bolden

# Disclaimer

This book has been written for information purposes only. Every effort has been made to make this book as complete and accurate as possible.

However, there may be mistakes in typography or content. Also, this book provides information only up to the publishing date. Therefore, this book should be used as a guide - not as the ultimate source.

The purpose of this book is to educate. The author and the publisher do not warrant that the information contained in this book is fully complete and shall not be responsible for any errors or omissions.

The author and publisher shall have neither liability nor responsibility to any person or entity with respect to any loss or damage caused or alleged to be caused directly or indirectly by this book.

# TABLE OF CONTENT

# INTRODUCTION

Social networking is unbeatable. It is a potent marketing channel that may change the game for any company. It gives us the flexibility to communicate on both a personal and professional level.

Business owners may use search media to improve search rankings, leads, sales, and traffic. This may be accomplished with little marketing cost. Beyond business, it's a cool platform for connecting with friends and loved ones.

Social media can be used to produce fantastic marketing pieces. Large brands like Skelton and Dell have successfully embraced social media to grow their customer base, brand awareness, and sales. No matter the size of your business, social media can be used to connect with your target market and strengthen your brand.

Customers and their demands dominate business in the modern world. Before making a purchase, people prefer to read referral reviews over those found on websites or in Google search results.

We must learn what others are saying about ourselves in order to follow the flow. You must actively engage in relevant communities in order to connect with and influence large populations. You must interact with social media to manage your online reputation. Social media marketing is essential if you want to expand your business and target a larger consumer base.

Social media marketing is the practice of driving website traffic via social media websites.

Social media marketing makes use of social media platforms to increase online visibility and promote goods and services. Social media platforms are helpful for creating social (and business) networks and for exchanging knowledge and ideas.

# CHAPTER 1

## How does social media marketing (SMM) work?

Social media is a platform that enables us to participate in social networking. We may share our posts on several social media channels to increase business exposure.

It is currently the best source of news, updates, marketing, education, and entertainment.

I am aware that you are prepared to jump right in and begin developing a social media strategy.

It is crucial that you comprehend what social media is and why so many people use it before we go with this. Let's begin with a definition. Wikipedia states that Online content created by people utilizing widely available and scalable publishing technology is known as "social media." In its most basic sense, social media is a shift in how people discover, consume, and share news, information, and material. It is the confluence of sociology and technology, changing monologues (one too many) into dialogues (many to many), and it is the decentralization of knowledge, converting people from avid readers into writers. Social media has gained a lot of popularity because it enables people to connect in the online world and form connections for personal, professional, and political purposes.

Wow, there is a ton of stuff there! Let's break it down into its three basic parts, which are publication, information dissemination, and connection building.
Social Media: A Publication Tool for Everyone

Social media is distinct from any other technology in history. It has created a modern-day renewal for a number of reasons, which are outlined here:

**Social media is online.**

Online social media is something that happens. It is a kind of communication that doesn't include in-person encounters, phone conversations, or foot traffic. Social media is thus location-independent, making it a useful component of any company's business strategy.

**Social media is user-generated.**

Content used to be something that a relatively small number of people created. Everyone consumed the content that journalists, TV anchors, movie directors, authors, radio DJs, and magazine editors produced. Everyone is now a publisher, and those who use the material are also the ones who make it.

## Social media is very accessible and scalable.

Social media is very accessible and understandable to the general public, which means that it has a large user base and offers several opportunities for businesses. Because social media is accessible, the tools for using it are simple and intuitive enough for the average person to use. There is no reason not to join, even if you don't currently use social media.

## Social media: A method of disguising information

Social media is the only available medium that is capable of sifting through information more quickly.

Here's why:

Social media refers to a change in how people discover, read, and share news, media, and content. Television and newspapers are no longer kings when it comes to filtering and disseminating news. Reading trending topics on Twitter and sharing a link to a friend's blog are two ways that people are more likely to stay up-to-date with the news.

More so than MSN's home page, social media is a fusion of social and technological factors.

Social media is user-controlled, which means that social media components play a significant role in any company's social media business strategy. The limits of social media are only established by the limitations of social media tool technology.

## Social media is a conversation.

Companies formerly engaged in a dialogue with their customers. Companies advertised their items on television or in print, and they watched to see whether sales increased in order to determine their success rates. Today, social media enables businesses to interact with their customers and get vital feedback and input as they craft their messages.

## Social media is democratizing of information

A company's marketing and sales departments were in charge of all information and messaging. With the decentralization of information, no one is in control of the message about a product or business anymore. Every company must participate in the convention or risk allowing users to speak for the organization.

## Social Media: A Tool for Relationship Building Through Sharing

Humans are interested in the fact that sharing is how they establish relationships. It may be discussing a hilarious TV moment or something that occurred in their own lives. Let's break sharing down into its component parts, as it is an essential part of social media:

## Social media involves individuals interacting with one another.

Every person may connect with others via social media; therefore, the majority of the messages that individual gets come from their network. Companies must understand how to communicate with their customers in order to spread the company message.

**Social media is for content readers who also act as content providers.**

Readers of content are not just consumers. Social media enables content readers to become content creators. Social media enables readers of material to share it with their own network of followers by posting or republishing the message on their own terms.

Social media is fostering relationships for personal, political, and commercial purposes.

Social media is more than just content or communication in a different format. Social media is all about connections. For businesses, social media is about developing a more personal relationship with end users in order to create a network around a service or product.
It is obvious that there are numerous aspects to social media, but the best way to comprehend them is to just use them. By this point, I hope you're eager to learn what social media can do for your business.

# CHAPTER 2

## Benefits of social media marketing

While many of the most popular social networking sites, including MySpace, Facebook, and Twitter, were initially thought of as platforms through which individuals could share with one another, these sites are quickly evolving into valuable tools for businesses in their efforts to strengthen their brands and reach out to potential customers. In addition to these advantages, social media marketing (SMM) gives firms the chance to:

- Helping others with knowledge, tools, and resources
- Create brand awareness.
- Develop trust among the online community.
- Create a following.

Convert followers into website visitors, and website visitors into customers.

The beauty of social media marketing (SMM) is that it is an inexpensive way to connect with people, and anybody can use it at any time.

To get the most out of this business tool, however, you'll need to invest some time in developing a plan of action and understanding how to start out on the right foot, keep your audience engaged, and gauge your success.

## Strategy for using social media

Social media and networking websites have been rapidly gaining popularity in recent years for one reason: they're entertaining.
Finding and forming meaningful connections with others who share your interests and passions is stimulating. Not only that, but he is far from being a

Instead of being a pointless distraction, it may be a very fruitful activity if you engage in it in a planned manner.

By using social media in a disciplined manner, you may greatly affect your visibility and reputation while also taking pleasure in the interactions that arise.
Setting goals. What action do you want the users of your network or your blog to take? What do you hope they will gain from their experience with you on social media?

Determine your audience. Most firms invest a

significant amount of time, money, and energy during the launch phase to identify their potential customers. Put this to good use by concentrating your social media efforts on the appropriate target demographic.

Know the image you want to project. Are you a liar, an authoritarian, or the go-to person? Establish your real-life profile and convey it in all of your social media and online networking activities.

Select your format. Post blogs using blog platforms like Word Press.

Blogger, among others.

## Starting Over

It's crucial to approach SMM with the proper mindset from the start. SMM may be a great way to connect with people, make friends and connections, and persuade them to visit your website, but it is a relatively new art. People can detect dishonesty and ulterior motives in milliseconds, even online; therefore, using SMM properly is essential.

**Give, and you will get.**

It's a mantra that you'll probably hear again in the social media world and might very well be the most crucial (and difficult) agreement to make. It cannot be stressed enough: every blog post, every article, and every interaction with you

Focus your social media interactions on how they benefit your audience, not your business.

It's time for you to start presenting yourself to the online community now that the assumptions about your motivations have been appropriately set. You can just choose one SMM strategy if you so choose, but using a variety of tools to increase your online presence is a more effective strategy. This resource focuses on these three:

- Social networking
- Blogging
- Content Sharing

## 1. Social networking

You may already be using social networking websites to stay in touch with friends and family. Twitter, Facebook, MySpace, LinkedIn, Bebo, and Friendster are some of the most popular sites right now because they are easy to use, ubiquitous, and have a wide range of applications and features that make using the sites fun. Additionally, there are a number of SMM websites that are particularly great for business objectives (Reddit, Digg, Del.icio.us, and StumbleUpon, to mention a few). Social networking contacts will also often recommend a few of their favorite SMM websites to you.

Spend some time up front creating your resume, which should include biographical information, a photograph, objectives, interests, knowledge, and other professional and personal affiliations. Use these themes in the social networking site's search feature to find people and organizations that share your interests and affiliations. Instead of sitting back and waiting for the conversations to begin, introduce yourself. Just like you would at a party or business convention, extend your hand to the online community.

Whether you're using a personal account, a business account, or both, be open and welcoming. Encourage your new acquaintances in the online community to think of you as a good neighbor and a resource.

## 2. Blogging

Blogs are a must-have for businesses looking to establish a presence online. Use blog posts on websites such as Word Press and others as a resource for others by regularly releasing new, unique content that is of interest to and useful to others. Your blog contributions will be far more significant and valuable if they are focused on sharing information and resources with others rather than criticizing your own products or disparaging the efforts made by your company.

However, directly, these posts help you establish your authority in your sector and provide readers with a good incentive to visit your website. Give readers a convenient method to contact you for more help and guidance, in addition to offering links to useful resources.

## 3. Content Sharing

This differs somewhat from blogging in that it encompasses not only sharing ideas and information via posts but also sharing material through other channels and content sharing websites:

- Press releases published in art form (PRWeb,

eReleases, PRNewswire)
- Images (via Flickr)
- Video (YouTube, Yahoo Video, Google Video)
- Whitepapers (www.del.icio.us)
- Presentations

Be careful about connecting with each of these methods.

Link back to your website from your blog, social networking page, or content sharing platform while also linking out to these SMM resources from your company website.

## Maintain your social media presence.

It may take some time to build up a following and see real-world results (read: "conversions") for social media marketing (SMM), depending on how much time you can set aside for it, but with consistent effort and perseverance, all that "paying forward" may pay off in a significant manner. Set aside time each day, even if it's only a few minutes, to keep up your social media presence, if at all feasible.

You could want to enlist the help of a friend, coworker, or online marketing partner to handle your

SMM campaign on a regular basis for you, or at the very least to keep up with it while you're out of town or bogged down. Some firms provide everything from simple blog posting services to copywriting services, so you can get professionally written content as well.

If it helps, make a list of the tasks you wish to complete:

- Monitor blogs and social media for activity.
- Respond to posts, questions, and comments on the wall.
- Post a new blog on a chosen subject.
- Find and add new contacts.

Results won't be seen immediately, but social media marketing (SMM) is in some ways a "you get out of it what you put into it" proposition. The more you can invest in the concept, the more likely it is that you will see profitable business outcomes.

# CHAPTER 3

## Drive more traffic from social media.

Although social media has the potential to be one of your biggest traffic sources, it also takes the most time and effort to manage. The occasional tweet or Facebook post is insufficient to change the outcome.

### 1. Do not forget the link or CTA.

It may seem obvious, but always add a link or call to action that leads back to your website. It not only increases traffic but also instructs your reader on what to do next.

No matter how much someone likes your brand, if you don't ask them to visit your website, make it easy for them to do so, and provide them with a compelling reason to do so, they are unlikely to do so. Therefore, always use social media as a teaser and provide a website link for further information.

On platforms like Instagram and Vine, doing this could be challenging, but you can always change it up and direct them to the link in your profile.

## 2. Always include a picture.

Using images in your social media postings is crucial when sharing content, particularly now that the majority of social media consumers use mobile devices.

Images help you draw in more attention since they are more attention-grabbing than text alone and take up more space in the timeline. Additionally, the ideal image may aid readers in visualizing what the material will be about and increase the "sharability" of a post.

### *Images boost engagement across the board.*

- Posts with images get 39% more interaction on Faccbook.
- LinkedIn posts with images get 98% more comments.
- Including images and/or videos in your Twitter posts may increase engagement by up to 200%.

## 3. Include social sharing buttons on your blog posts.

It's great when you can generate a lot of traffic via

your social media channels, but it's even better when other people do it for you.

If your website doesn't already have social sharing buttons, you can be missing out on a lot of social media traffic that comes from people who are currently reading your blog.

Social sharing buttons are those eye-catching buttons you see at the top or bottom of blog entries that allow you to share the page directly on the social media channel of your choice.

They provide convenience for your buyer persona and act as a non-pushy tool that promotes social sharing. Sumome and Shareaholic are two of the most popular and cost-free social sharing tools.

## 4. Use paid promotion or sponsored content.

The quickest way to get more traffic from social media is via paid promotion.

Paid promotion, or "sponsored content," feeds the flames when you're using a traditional social media strategy. You may experiment with various targeting choices (such as region, gender, industry, and interests on most profiles) to help draw in new audiences and increase traffic.

B2B marketers will probably have to pay to be seen as the business models of social media platforms evolve. Facebook has been operating in this manner for a few years, and with the recent introduction of algorithmic timelines on Twitter and Instagram, this trend is probably here to stay.

## 5. Be involved and active.

Too many B2B brands are guilty of failing to regularly update their social media. The only way to keep your followers interested is to provide updates and communicate with individuals often. Otherwise, they could forget about you.

When we tell B2B marketers that they aren't active enough on social media, their minds immediately picture a young girl who is addicted to her phone and constantly updates on her every move. Then, we reassure them that being active doesn't require them to devote their lives to social media.

Actually, a few postings every day are sufficient to complete the check.

**Here is a simple yet effective daily schedule:**

- Updates 1-3 that are not promotional
- Share 1-3 pieces of content from your brand.
- Share 1-3 helpful articles from other businesses, influencers, or new websites.
- Spend around 5 to 10 minutes responding to questions and comments.

**Determine your success.**

Gauging the success of an SMM campaign isn't always an exact science, but there are methods to determine whether or not you are reaching the correct people. You may utilize analytical tools such as Google Analytics, which is free, and Omnituret are used to count the number of visitors.

You can see who is visiting your social media pages, how long they stay there, how many pages they see, if they go over to your business website, and more.

Many of the social networking and SMM websites you use have tools for evaluating the volume and kind of activities you are attracting with your profile and your actions via that profile.

However, whether you have tools or not, you may still

see certain trends on your own. Who are the viewers and commenters on your posts and wall postings? Do these individuals represent your target audience, or are they influential figures in your sector? Are you seeing an increase in traffic to your own website, or are you getting more requests for information or sales? How many people have subscribed to your RSS feeds?

## Basic SMM dos and don'ts

Do...

- Be honest, open, and impartial while using social media and networking tools.
- Address issues that have significance for your target audience. Prioritize them.
- Provide original content and a fresh perspective.
- Pay attention to your contacts and respond in a manner that is meaningful and practical for them.
- Give them a way to contact you for more support.
- Give links to other helpful resources.
- Remember that social media is about what you can do for others.

Don't...

- Wait for an invitation. Speak with your audience.
- Sneak inside a storefront. This is a turn-off for anyone seeking advice and information.
- Talk excessively about yourself or your business. Keep your audience's interest at the forefront of your thoughts.
- Forget to keep an eye on your feedback and respond quickly.
- Overlook the significance of having a reliable housing provider. You want a dependable server infrastructure that can cope with increased traffic.

## Viral Advertising

Most businesses are aware of the advantages of utilizing social media for viral marketing, but few know how to carry out such a campaign. First, let's clarify what a variety marketing campaign is.

It's a frequent misperception that viral marketing messages need millions of page views or to attract thousands of followers in a short period of time to be effective. Unfortunately, very few small to medium-sized businesses will ever experience this sort of success because their markets are too limited or their products are specialized. Many marketing campaigns are simply persuasive messages that expose common behaviors, make use of already-existing networks, and can be efficiently transmitted from one person to another on a large scale. A variety of marketing campaigns' success metrics must include the company's strengths, resources, and rivals.

Now that you know what a viral marketing plan is, you may be wondering what causes websites, posts, and videos to go viral. Every viral marketing campaign is supported by three components, and without at least some of each, success is unlikely. These three components are a sizable user base, a noteworthy message, and a convincing justification for disseminating that message.

## Components: Building a Large User Base

There are only two ways to reach a large group of people: devote a lot of time or invest a lot of cash. If your company is interested in social media, it's usually because you want to reach a broad user base without having to spend a lot of money on advertising. One thing to keep in mind with social media is that it is not "free." Most of the tools are free, and there is plenty of free literature explaining how to use social media for your business. Unfortunately, the truth of social media is that it requires time—much more time than, say, creating a banner advertisement. For businesses with many staff, time costs money as well.

The good news is that right now is the ideal time to start. There are some straightforward guidelines for developing an online presence across many different networks, and with only a short daily time investment, you may use social media for your business.

# Conclusion

With more than 70% of internet users active on social networks and an average daily use of at least one hour, we must draw the conclusion that social networks have evolved into a kind of reality in which people interact, communicate, and are obviously trustworthy. We also need to be aware that more than 60% of those users access social networks via mobile devices, with strong indicators that this percentage will only rise in the coming years.

In such a society, we must acknowledge that social networks are a new reality that has permeated the business sphere as well. Over 90% of marketers claim they are or will be utilizing social networks for business, and more than 60% of them claim to have gained new customers and increased traffic on social networks.

According to research published by business professionals and marketers, businesses may greatly benefit from using social networks, which is why doing so has become standard practice. This is why social media marketing is no longer seen as being in question but has instead evolved into an essential component of the commercial sector.

## About The Author

Andrew K. Bolden is a renowned Sales Acceleration Specialist with over 15 years of experience in sales and marketing. He is widely recognized for his ability to help sales organizations achieve peak performance fast by optimizing talent, leveraging training to cultivate high-performance sales culture, developing leadership and coaching skills, and applying more effective organizational design.

Andrew is passionate about empowering sales professionals to achieve their full potential, and he has worked with some of the world's most successful companies to help them achieve significant sales growth. He has a deep understanding of the sales process, and he has developed a range of innovative tools and strategies that have proven to be highly effective in accelerating sales growth and improving the overall performance of sales teams.

# Other Books By Andrew K Bolden

- WANT TO DROP SHIP?: Step-By-Step Guide To Boost Your E-commerce Business with Dropshipping
- CUSTOMER RELATIONSHIP MARKETING: Effective CRM Techniques That Will Keep Your Customers Coming Back.
- Money saving Tips: 15 Top Ways To Handle Every MONEY SAVING Challenge With Ease.
- SELL YOUR HOME : 101 TIPS FOR SELLING YOUR HOME WITH OR WITHOUT REAL ESTATE AGENT
- EXCELLENT COACHING BUSINESS: BELIEVE IN YOUR COACHING SKILLS BUT NEVER STOP IMPROVING, LEARN TO BUILD A SUCCESSFUL ONLINE COACHING BUSINESS
- THE MAGIC OF NETWORK MARKETING: 70 Proven Ways to Generate More Leads to your Network
- The Wonder Book: How To Find A Niche And Make Money
- The Ultimate Sales Funnel: A Step By Step Guide On How To Build A Killer Online Business and Create Massive Amounts Of Wealth Starting Today
- Built For Duty: Claim Your Power, Live Fearlessly And Become Unstoppable To Win At Anything You Set Your Mind To.
- INSTAGRAM MARKETING: The Ultimate Instagram Marketing Guide To Boost Your Business
- Unheard Ways To Achieve Greater PUBLIC SPEAKING: Master The Art To Speak Like Pro - Get Rid Of Social Anxiety And Become More Confident

- Attraction Marketing: How To Stop Working for Money and Make Money Work for You.
- From An Idea To Reality: How To Handle Every ENTREPRENEUR Challenge With Ease Using These Tips
- SOCIAL MEDIA MARKETING: 51 Proven Social Media Marketing Hacks To Boost Your Business
- Canyon Of Intellectual Being: Powerful Ways To Sharpen Your Brain
- Map To Success: 10 Simple Ways To Make Your Marketing Plan Successful
- THE FIVE R's: Your Basic Guide To Understand TIME MANAGEMENT, PROJECT MANAGEMENT, ATTENTIVE MANAGEMENT, EFFECTIVE ENVIRONMENT, SETTING GOALS, ORGANIZATION AND LEADERSHIP
- The Wealth Mindset: How Rich People Think and How You Can Too
- The 6-Figure Blogger: A Step-by-Step Guide to Making Money Online
- Calm Your Mind And Grow Your Wealth: Understanding The Evolution Of Entrepreneurship And Building Leadership Skills To Succeed In Business
- From 9 to 5 To Your Own Boss: Building Your Dream Internet Business
- From Zero to Six Figures: The Ultimate Guide to Building a Profitable Coaching Program
- The Online Coaching Revolution: Create Profitable Courses, Books, and Videos to Earn Money While You Sleep

# One Last Thing…

Dear Reader,

I hope you enjoyed reading this book and found it to be valuable for your needs. As an author, it means a lot to me when readers take the time to leave a review on Amazon. Your feedback not only helps me improve my writing but also helps potential readers decide if this book is right for them.

If you have a few minutes to spare, I would greatly appreciate it if you could leave a review on Amazon. Your honest opinion can help other readers make informed decisions and can make a real difference in the success of this book.

To leave a review, simply search for the book title and my name on Amazon.com, and select the book from the search results. Once you have navigated to the book's page, scroll down to the review section and share your thoughts on the book.

Rest assured that every single review is personally read and appreciated by me. Your feedback is crucial in helping me understand what worked well and what could be improved upon in future editions. Thank you in advance for your support and for taking the time to leave a review.

Best regards,

Andrew K. Bolden